THE TRUE HEIGHT OF THE EAR

.

IAIN GALBRAITH

The True Height
of the Ear

ARC
PUBLICATIONS
2018

Published by Arc Publications,
Nanholme Mill, Shaw Wood Road
Todmorden OL14 6DA, UK
www.arcpublications.co.uk

978 1911469 29 2 (pbk)
978 1911469 30 8 (hbk)

Design by Tony Ward

Cover painting:
'La Lune Bleue' by Francis West
© Francis West

ACKNOWLEDGEMENTS
The author is grateful to the editors of the following
journals and anthologies, where some of the poems in
this book first appeared: *Akzente*, *The Allotment: New
Lyric Poets*, *Best Scottish Poems 2005*, *Edinburgh Review*,
Irish Pages, *Modern Poetry in Translation*, *New Writing*,
New Writing Scotland, *PN Review*, *Poetry Review*, *Qualm*,
The Times Literary Supplement, *The Warwick Review*.
'Translation of the God' was commissioned by
the Cultural Foundation of the Canton of Thurgau,
Switzerland, for the tenth Frauenfeld Poetry Festival,
September 2009.
'Passing the Steading', 'Stellar State', 'Strange
Harvest' and 'In This Way' were set to music by Ulrich
Leyendecker and first performed on 2 April 2016 at the
Orangerie, Wiesbaden, Germany.

Editor for the UK & Ireland
John Wedgewood Clarke

For Leonie and Simon

CONTENTS

For I have been before now a boy and a girl,
a bush and a bird, and a mute fish in the sea.

EMPEDOCLES

the Here and Now (…) has not yet even entered time and space.
Instead, the contents of this most immediate nearness still
ferment entirely in the darkness of the lived moment as the real
world-knot, world-riddle.

ERNST BLOCH

The void they haunt is living earth

THE UNCLAIMED ACRE

Few who come here (and they
these days are few) will
know this place

by the voice of an acre nobody
claims, a useless patch,
its walls and rusted fences

sheering Wade's old
road from alders and tussocks
of matted Deschampsia, boulders

of Prussian blue. There,
you might ask, so what? Or
to what end? And where

now is the *Harmony of the Heath*,
the dancing Fern? When I
was a girl I woke to the rasp

of reapers scything the hay,
the fighting men of Old
Norway crossing the field,

and a Polish navvy died
in the bothy next door.
This is the spot where Samuel

Coleridge, *disappointed*
and *shoeless*, made sure
to turn away and walked

from our abiding rain
and savage folk to liberty.
Mounds under moss outline

the plots of some of the tales
I wish to tell. Over the
hill by the pier I've already

assembled the fish, a babe
at arms, my first kiss, and
ladies in high-laced boots.

There will be a something for every-
soul: the nightmare, ices,
an ancient parrot, and whether.

I'll not forget the girl
who drowned in the burn, the storm,
the wrecked plane in the wood,

or the white stag's eye:
desire paths and doorways
to the acre nobody claims.

VOICE

in memory of Francis West

The man was half
a mile long, tipping the dunes
into the fluted fields.

Behind him the sun,
the agile one, discreet,
stalking the jagged rocks.

Lazy-beds stretched
pink beneath the skirts
of the ingoing squall,

and a flock of plover,
starved for a week, gorged
on the thawing land.

Turned-to for an instant,
lost, a hailing voice
far out to sea.

THE TRUE HEIGHT OF THE EAR

I drew aside the branches of a tree
and peered into the light. I saw the faces,
fair enough to me and odd
how tall some were – or how, a rising tide
of perished flesh my family was coy:
the men behind white beards while sullen
women stared askance,
biding by the safer walls as if their god

of rectitude could smell in me some dance
or pool of sin, clasping to my breast a boy.
And how the older maids
were framed in holes, perhaps the squares of doors,
while mounted round the teeming room a style
in hand-me-downs was labelled *Pindi,
Kars, H.M.S. Thule,*
or just *A weekend stalking on the bens,*

Sir Ivor shaving through a Brownie lens.
Above us hung a throng of dazzling blades:
kukri and skean-dhu,
assegai, finger-nail, hyuck and guandao,
each as sharp as a fish-knife. Was the curse
of sabres tempered by our homely quilts
and appliqués? Had
the clash of cutlass chilled that air with truth? –

all this for setting in some Adirondack
rail inspector's hut, but how the heck the shack
all packed with keg
and horn got to that place I could not guess.
My uncles fought at brag around this board.
A dirk-brawl stained its ear-height edge –

a blood I swear I heard.
Then Auntie Bella read a yellowed letter,

asking if my Dad had thought he'd kick the can
or what had come of you or yet your mother
if he had, you who know
so many taken in your time and no
foretelling who must go. Now, she warned me,
was the pressing season, respite none
for all eternity –
and was I not to Death as liable as the next?

On such a ledge I'd never cared to dangle,
grabbed our younger tight above the elbow
making out I'd oh,
forget my head, my thoughts all in a fankle.
Backing off the stoop I watched their faces fall:
left something in the van –must go,
have to – sorry, be back
soon… And still in view of pendent steel

am dragging him across the pitching stage,
yelling to the bigger boy who's now in tears
to get the hell in the car,
and spindles skidding soon am churning down
the dirt-front sideways. It's time to shoot
my parabellum through this ceiling, Son –
and moving on we'll chew
on olden days, your mother slaving in the kitchen,

gutting haddock on the day the boiler blew,
and in the winter of this tale her liver failing.
I've always wished you well –

I write to you in hope you will recall
my loyal letters when you lay my grey head
in the grave. If only we could throw our
arms around each other
what a comfort we would have in this place then.

PASSING THE STEADING

If tups and fank are all but ghosts
the void they haunt is living earth:
the way damp worsted rubbed on stone
or shapes we work dissolve in rain.

THE BONHILL DIVAN

i. m. Isabella MacAllister & James Galbraith,
married 5.11.1819, Bonhill

A vista wrought for a royal jaunt would likely sleek
our Lord Blantyre who henceforth saw his pleasure's commerce
entered to the darkening glist of Delft and Venice –
sequestrated promise downset in Claudian willows,
an umbrous Bowling canal. Dumbarton Rock's the smirr

of ages fast in erd and stane, a warrandice
to steamboats coursing for the grand emporium's heart.
On my lap's a westward view from Milton or Dalnottar,
clouds ablaze like fiery garments over the Clyde.
The mind's eye flees, reaches, squints, hurries

back with dyers, printers, mills, the blackened grass:
a weavers' road that hurtles through the mutable estates
where wick and virtue flare to fife and drums,
the torchlit scintill of three hundred shattered panes.
The late train to Tarbet gently halts and hums –

a voice regrets the hindrance left across the rails
(two boys, one me, later reported
scaling this embankment with an iron bed).
I return to my page of po-faced sheep – Arcadia complete
with penny wedding, tittling billie, the guidwife in her mutch.

AUSPICE

First, raise your eyes. Look up into the sky.
EURIPIDES

Through the window I watch the buzzard
mobbed from a branch by a pair of jays.
I am here to remember my mother,
who no longer knows where she lives

or her name, but wake to find my own
son's head wrapped in a sheet
in my arms. There has been some error
surely? Cries the raptor, fainter,

gone is the house you founded once in brick
but not even you after so many lifetimes
know who you are or why, when summer slips
and the light grows silver and thin,

a gossamer chorus flies.

RETURN TO A DIFFERENT PLACE

Surf dins on the rocks at the point
and a tiny figure gleams in my tray.

She pulls me along as she always does,
laughing, waving, the tail of her stripy

scarf flapping in the wind as she turns
to sprint for the moss-covered rigs.

At the edge of the field her shadow
thins and bleeds from the sharper zone

(she drops out of sight, half twists
away, appears again on the path)

and how am I meant to hold the pace,
such icy haste in my darling girl

as back and forth and back she swings
across the barbed-wire fence.
                                    Blistering

into focus now
the singular thing we already know

smudges the arch of the branch – soon
it will feed from the edge, searing

a path to the heart unchecked,
repeating all it sees.

All of this and all its opposite

HACKING INTO FOREVER

How can a soul be a merchant? What relation to an
immortal being have the price of linseed, the fall of butter …
WALTER BAGEHOT

A glacial pass led me down to the middle
where spent salmon lay in rows in the shallows of a lake,
bruised souls. No cry was heard

the day I torched the tomes of Atlanta – *Anomura*,
mute hermit crabs, recall the act. *Nyassa*,
Poseidonia, La Nouvelle Caledonie – there is no end

to the work of erasure. For see my eyeless lovers shine
and all our children and their children's children
gather on the roof. In search of myself I enter the Eocene.

OWLETS

The moment we curved into the alley of planes –
our attention wrenched from the winking lights of towns,
which, like swarms of glow-worms or
the campfires of an army waiting for dawn in the hills,
had floated across the shallow darkness when we took
the bends – I saw them, felt the jolt, registered,
without knowing how, the simulacrum
of a longer story blindly taking
its course.
          Three tiny sentinels,
hunched in their greatcoats under the canopy
of leaves, miniature protagonists in a theatre
of war, were stationed at regular intervals
along my side of the central marker. Unflinching
in the headlights three pairs of eyes had glowed
and seemed to stare at us. Fledglings, I told
myself, tumbled too early from the nest and
marked for death: guardians at the tunnel's mouth.
I stopped, walked back to the site of the carnage
and threw their mangled bodies in a ditch,
the warmth of their viscera still on my hands
until I found the cloth. Driving away

and for all the days that followed,
the thought of returning to smooth the plumage
of carcasses picked from the peppery tar
would not leave me in peace. I had understood at once,
had seen them too late – and between these poles
was one of a species who knowingly meets release.

THE CATALOGUE OF SHIPS

the ones who (...)
fly with a shriek over the streams of Okeanos
bringing slaughter and death to Pygmy men
ILIAD, 3, 4-6

The tide is sizzling with rain
The sails are counted and gone
The town lies razed in the dunes
Cranes take the war abroad

The clips go round and round
The surf is silvery-tongued
Sleepless recorders are counting
Pygmies torn by the cranes

Satellites cross the empyrean
Endless the battle begun
Cranes in the phalanx screaming
The heroes are counted and done

The wintering cranes above
The winter of battle below
The news goes round and round
The cost of a wind has soared

Endless the desert Ocean
Carcasses countless as grass
The dead can hear the wings
The shrieking cranes are gone.

BRONZE HELMET FROM POMPEII

First century AD, Height 46 cm, British Museum

1

For when a war is in the world, because
the war is yours and mine and enters every
pore, my room is like a dreary poet's
stanza where the stillness rhymes with kills
and sadness and a little apple tree,
dizzied by the looping swallows, and horses
muzzling salt-flowers softly from the bricks of
a barn, are ciphers glimpsed through a visor.

2

I dreamed we were a family of stateless
dolphins. Our boots were heavy with mud
and rubble and a cautious wall-eye watched me
as we struggled ashore. All morning they
sprayed the sunflowers from the air, and later in
the valley the jagged reports of a gun
tangled with echoes from the hill. Three doves
fled between the pines. Now there are none.

REVERSAL

*Nadie come naranjas
bajo la luna llena.*
         FEDERICO GARCIA LORCA

In the window
the valley glows

like a silver bowl –
silhouettes

at the threshold,
a new clenched noise.

The spill of shadows
creeps through the rooms

to the stone-anchored
roofs at the back.

Moments later
what was here before

tells us only
that nothing stays the same:

the deal table
overturned in the kitchen,

the cart climbing heavily
behind the house

through cork woods
and ripening maize,

the donkey snorting
under clanking pots,

a pannier of hens.
In the ravine,

framed by lies,
the lost man's pale face.

The moon sails –
the man is nobody,

in his hands
the blue fruits gleam.

CRY

One balmy evening as we idled on the terrace
with glasses of waterish red, a nightjar showed
among the thickets and osiers between the ruined dovecot
and an acre abutting the church march. Here,
not many decades earlier, some pieces of chantry
furniture, once secreted to elude the rage of the ravening
peuple, then forgotten, were found by an English lady
planting her sage and thyme. The nightjar itself
did not come to light on that summer's eve, or rather,
it did not strictly speaking *show*, or not as a bird
whose voice and name merged with a shape. Instead it was
only the cry, detached from word or concept,
much as the distinct horizon of a word, with its comely
hill-tops, factories, copses or spires – albeit sprung
less from a singular event than from the generic
constraints of its provenance – will sometimes wait
to reveal the shape it takes on the white of a page
until after we have heard its sound on another's lips. The hoarse
churr of the nightjar, in any case, sounded only
once in the policies of that eighteenth-century manor.
For a moment it was there and then – like the fighter-jet
passing low above the sparsely populated reach
of Burgundy where the old house stood, described
by the one who identified the rasping call of the obscure bird
as *training for deployment overseas* – was gone, without
our glimpsing as much as its silhouette over the church woods.

OPPOSITES

for J. D. G. (1927-1998)

Sitting in the promenade car-park
with the front doors
                              swung wide open
and rocking now and then on their hinges
as the wind gusts
                              through the spaces

I drift from the radio chatter,
drawn to the undertow's
hiss and groan:

the waves smash pebble on pebble,
sucking back
                      a slatted fruit-box,
a ball, or maybe a buoy,
                                    the surf then,
with its whisper of carrier bags,

hauling up against the drag –
and, for all their weight, with such ease –
your final words to me.

Across the firth, through clouds
as dark and heavy this morning
as Victorian furniture,
a crystal light is breaking.

Their stark whiteness
                              outshining
a flurry of gulls,
gannets plunge

into their moments to come,
scattering all aside
spearing into the glassy surge
lean necks straining for sustenance
through the resisting pitch.

I know your words
meant all of this
and all its opposite.

FIND ME, EAT ME

The immunologist has heard the signal
whispered by an apoptotic cell in peril:
need to terminate. Before an oleander
bloom she holds her quizzing glass. Her tears
will surely end this story soon: *explore,*
you must resolve precisely what life is…

Outside the kitchen's square of light
a pipistrelle will flap and hiss all night,
one wing trapped by the garage door.

SIBLINGS

No breath passes the shutter
and no wind ruffles the sail –
scenes taken in June on the river,

girls in debate, their pale arms
like swans' necks against the blue keel.
The sleeper shifts under his sheet,

the boy rides on down the street.
Will the general cast his die?
If the dream has a brother,

now that Gaul has a governor...
The water's coils blacken
and bleed to their kind in the sky.

Sleep is the victor with a helmet,
its horse-crest blossoming like flame.
His twin has troubled the dreamer,

his persistence threatens a border –
feet stamp, short swords
tabor the leather-covered shields –

in no time a scatter of bullets
pocks the wash-house wall.
The ricochets will stop at his skin,

but the boy is no longer there.
The wheels on his bike still spin,
his absence lives on in your eye.

BEST MAN DEAD

The lime-kiln's tumble in a drum of wind,
a dovecot slipping its marches to roll
to a field full of crushed clams – accidental
here as the scurrying shadows of clouds
is the man who strains with a yellow pail,
the turnstone's piping beyond the links...

Two knights of solemn vow, small bodies
twisted apart by the mortar-blast of their choice,
smile in calamity's face, inviolable now,
their closed eyes and lips candescent with return.

POLECAT

Returning home in the icy hours
my hatchback threads the glinting Milky Way;
a galaxy's reflections sparkle under my wheels –
hero, maiden, dragon, a garden in full bloom –
and crossing the avenue, snout and tail,
looping the headlamps between the Bears,
the fire-eyed polecat flees to his black hole.
                                        By dawn
a little girl is standing by my bed in tears:
the horseman has come for her through the snow.
Wee in her bonnet, green coat, dazed,
my mother waits on the hoar-feathered lawn,
her soft throat seared by the ionizing rays.

ELEGY FOR A HEDGEHOG

for J. M. G. (1928-2005)

How light you were on your deathbed,
and your breathing was just like a sparrow's
      after striking the glass.
By the next morning you were lost to us
      if you are not here still.
And I remember the moment during the vigil

through those long hours
with the cold clamped on our barely feeling limbs –
      that vacant sound-shape close-by, loud,
like a rasping or foot's dragging
      across the flags in the yard.
Assailed by lung-worm perhaps

(but we thought only of the death-room's rattle)
its eerie voice had come to our door
      in the silence of the early morning –
a wheezing hedgehog crouching there,
      unexplained by the lamp in the porch,
its presence obscure and not

yet a part, in that hour, of what we would know.
I thought instead of a different wildness
      when once we had lain awake all night in the wind
and were unable to gauge the havoc we saw
      when we stepped outside next morning.
The great pandemonium had passed,

and the sun was wan and sick,
rocks and alders looked to be floating
            in a rolling netherworld,
the waves and clouds stained black,
            boats still dragging at their moorings.
How that wind with its scythe and dreadful shouting

had slashed through the beeches at Bandry –
from Firkin to Fruin lay their cadavers.
            Above an upturned tractor in the field
pink gashes had opened in the sky
            and lurching crows jagged through
while the loch unfurled its scrolls.

And still you lie on your deathbed,
attired in a threadbare flesh,
            taken under our unshielding roof:
your heart a failing branch
            and our remnant too weak in the gusts
of this endless devastation.

ACHERONTIA

Above a bloom of grey-washed eaves
the cries of fearful children thread
the sky, and who knows why or when

they once began. – A mile-high blade
of fire lances the plain, and in
its after-burn the barges swing

across the stream, the hill-tops shine,
and even now the flight of cranes
is pressing south, while through

the steaming dust and rain a hawk-moth
jigs along the hollow street
beneath the dripping walnut leaves.

STRANGE HARVEST

In this country where to journey south
is not to find your story told in marble
alps of water crush a sleeping town.

I have spent all day in wanhope on this pier;
racked across the dry cornea of the sky
the twilight rays are gathered to a sheaf.

And then we were lifted, waking late from snippets of dreams,
from lips and deceases, chickens with cheeses, like a rabbit here,
a cricket not there that rises at last to its window song
we stirred to rickshaws and ratchets, wrinkles that fizzed or
    dissolved:
their divings and swirlings, their sheer of loops over five lemon
    trees.
Here for an instant we rose to the swarm, to the hundreds of how
many feeding and gathering, or tripping and up for the lick of it,
their kinky cross-patch tweets in the last-minute schoolings
of kids with twists whose crazy parabolas, twitching for biscuits,
had spun off the earth and were lost, each a toolbox of kickings.
This was a backstory cheerily ours over globes that were
    chechens
of ripeness, yellow and green in this light, such stickits and
    lychees
observed by a mischpoke of rooks in the willows and pitchy pines:
we were touched and keen for a state that could raise us to their
    cusp.
Might the lych-gate open, and we stand amongst them quickened?
We were holding hands, all girded and willing, while they were
    leaving,
reaching, already flipped away, from their quincunx, catches
    and visit.

SAW

All day it roared, nor did it bellow
with open-mawed bravour, but mewed
as if through parcel tape, the tentered tongue
lopped again, and this beside your fair-faced
brickwork mansions. Soon the grander fragments
toppled into the tufa ravine. The neighbours hung
on window-cushions to watch, their tears streaking
the pebble-dash as they wondered where on earth
the owls and rooks would roost hereafter. I filed away
their forms and got on the phone to you, architect
of it all. The world has seen your plaster shiver;
before the window I scarcely glance at now
an unknown river zags across the plain.

TRANSLATION OF THE GOD

The 'God Tamangur' is a stone pine wood, the highest of its kind in Europe ('god' is the Romansh word for forest). Situated in Lower Engadine in Eastern Switzerland it is linked to a potent myth: it is said the Romansh language will survive only for as long as the Tamangur forest continues to grow.

They came out of the heavens,
those hackers of shoulder and shin,
took a sighting of all that I was.
They came in the evening before the sun
retired to the back of the crags.

They fed and I was overset,
without witness rendered to a leafless country
where I must die as they live.

I do not speak as I did at home.
I do not speak as if I were lying,
dead or dying, on these paper-thin slopes.

They keep me in holy places,
talking to me daily;
in silence I answer the questions
they cannot cease to ask.

We have seen your ways, so they say,
dividing and dividing again, giving form
to our thrones, our armies, all our holy orders.
In the bareness of our mountains
spate-water follows your behest,
forking, wild to desert its parents
on the steep flanks of the fell.

We have watched your green-throated birds
hop through the spirals of our substance:
dendrites flood with your sap,
our families descend through your limbs.

We have given you time.
In return you have filled our archives,
growing names for the jade-metalled roads
that criss-cross our children's wrists.
Your ring-works tell our story.
We are the bearers
of the shapes you make,
the reason your fingers
draw cracks in the lighting sky.

This they say to me –
an elegy on the face of the orphaned earth.
They say it with my words.

FOR A MARGIN

The zigzag hand of a sanderling racing the rim –
two pale ounces of headlong rush, wanting a hinder toe.

Teeth and tongues of the snowline
and this whistling gate: all the north-easterly will allow.

THE DUNE-COMPASS

Needle in a horse-shoe, tip of the marram,
bending to scribble the jagged tale of the wind
on the sand, lend me your skills:

show me the hour of death, point when they hurry
to flee the land (bowing your head as the bunting
brushes your nib and leaves by the eastern gate).

In this way, alight, we follow

FROM THE TRAIN

after Eugenio Montale

Snow-geese had never come this far.
When I leant out of the window
there they were, guzzling behind the shack
left empty and sore the year
the northbound track was looped
around the wayside platform. In vain
I search for them now among the flocks
of foraging birds. Is that all
you wanted to say? But I am blind
to everything else as the down
of your letter flutters from my hand.

MEANWHILE

Midday August on the brink of sleep and the two
sapling larches, six foot and decrepit
in this heat, are barely leaning, their roots loosed out
to a desert breeze; two adjacent, less
like you and me, stronger, similar in stature, anchored
in the cracks, divide an unscathed section of asphalt
from the morning rawness, from the broccoli

gone to yellow along the tracks. It is a local line
and stopped without intent. I know it
for a moment sinking to another moment and five minutes
longer for this half-hour standstill,
for turnip blossom you would not believe, spurge
and tansy pushing through the siding reinforcements
then nothing, then a onetime greenhouse in its unseen

darkens. This is the disconnected decked with brittle
plastic sheeting, and in the quasi-
parting distance and the supermarket's tiling
a car's reflection flashes up
like a memory of homing doves. But now we're moving out,
observed by a hare in the wrecks of the maize,
alert, and delivered to a land that cannot respond.

ARRHYTHMIA

This I will say in memory of memory,
not mine alone, but all,
for surely the stretching snow-waste
fields were no less empty
on the day when first you pedalled
past me on the crown of your years,
at the bridge's keystone throwing a glance
over your shoulder, skirt and scarf
forever, now, riding the breeze? And not
because you had chosen me, nor
for any hope that we might call
the world to the pivot where our single
paths converged, our candle flaring,
did my heart miss a beat, but because
your balance faltered, your tyre misled
by a crack in the road, because
of this and the river stopping,
and the library's windows always ablaze
in winter shining, their surface blank,
like so many unread books.

QUAIL SONG

after Horace

The outlook for the winter months had now reversed –
the herded waves reared up and left
a tribe of fishes lodged in the tops of the elms,
the storms drove wolves from the heights.

Do you fancy we trembled with fright?
We yearned not once for city lights.
Instead in groaning woods we thanked
each dawning day, the blaze we plied

with logs and wrapped in blankets
drank from the Sabine jar. When springtime
came the pylons floated high above
the haze and but for a white-cap far

to north the snow soon burned away.
One evening carefree, close by the stream
she grasped my wrist – a voice sang out
in the corn: *wet-my-feet* they'd called

them on the farm where she was born.
Deep in the sedges reeled the kinglet wren
and marking a lull between incoming planes
ice-melt sighed on a stone.

CEYX AND HALCYONE

Cabbage-whites tumble across the breeze
and limbs twine through a moss-choked lock
where the wavy seams of spring-race and stream
run awash in the shadows: here
are flames of origin, the robes of a river-god's
whisper, the whirlpool, eddies and rock. Close
as peril the trapped source leaps, the sun
shatters, fountains ply scorn-gold. A splinter
burns across the surface, dreamt and gone.
Dragonflies mime her drowning rufous and blue.

RIVER AND MOON

after Su Tung-Po

Later dazed in evening rose
her eyes gleamed like the ancient locks
where melting asphalt glowed on sleepers
in the scorching heat and shining steel
swirled through the closing gates. The doves
our hostel shutters startled clattered
out across the square, and as I gazed

her shimmering skin, all bathed in moonlight,
poured between my sheets. In such a dawn,
amid the bales and drums, the guards in serge
had watched us while we joined a barge
at Varna, the port where vexed
by hope I'd crept in darkness from our bed
and trembling by my candle traced

these letters from a scroll. The strokes,
as Doctor Liu explained, portrayed a greater
river surging east and tearing at its banks –
and how in the lee of ancient ramparts where
the teeth of Zhou's Red Cliff had stabbed
the sky stood smiling Qiao, his bride,
and foam swelled up like snowdrifts

as surly waves assailed the fortress walls.
Was the dream my own or was it hers,
or yet Doctor Liu's? With her dashing silken
scarf, her plume fan shoulder-poised,
I'd seen her jest and tease while tall
masts burned… And though my heart
begins to pound as Zhou relives the fray,

my head is white as gosling down,
for long ago the river scoured all trace
of heroes' deeds. I raise the slats again
and welcome morning grey – but is not this
Zhou's moon on water through the leaves?
Why is all so fleeting? From the dregs
I pour a cup to river and moon.

DAQQUQA TAT-TOPPU

(Maltese name for a hoopoe)

for Christiane

Paladin caller of the waking hours
he bustles among the pine-nuts,
bathing in dust, probing the dead,
an augur in the pathways of ants.

Cavalier of these parts he nodded
and left his name – when you threw
back the shutters he took his hat,
hid in the cloak of the sea.

We looked out for him daily.
The islands sparkled in showers
of untried light – his morning, ours.

How could we doubt his return?
Who sits with us at this table
covering my hand with your own?

DOCTOR SUBTLE

a visit to the final resting place of John Duns Scotus

You cannot imagine a yellow spot and nothing else
she says, brought up in the plaza's turba and spill.
I think of a lolly, but her thirty-two-million-mile
neuronal coil consists not of think but of cells.

Perhaps after this we shall never speak again – I mean,
my basal ganglia have absorbed too much of a shock.
Majuscules, all Greek, drop mumbling out of the sky –
the delta flopped on the boy's head is a D's cone.

Someday I will show you my power-point display
of re-entry patterns filmed in the dynamic core
of a dog, but now keep watching that orb, forever
meeting the dark, forever bleeding away.

BLACKBIRD

for Anona

You read at a window,
beyond your shoulder
     the white

ridge of a wall   ports
in a snow-laden
fir. You

invite me to picture
          a layered
molecule of graphite. The atoms,

         you posit, are firmly
joined, but the tension
      that keeps the layers

together is pliant
enough to let them
          slip

and slide, holding
        because they yield.
The tip of my finger

      traces pencilled lines
to the lithesome
        dark of the word

at the top of the page –
            the jet of her eye
alert in the conifer's

haven, the brush
of a wing as she whirls
from the heavy

            branch.

CHERRY TIME

It's light past seven when the door bell rings.
    In no time ago we went
        plucking cherries under the stacking planes –

the two girls on their tiptoes, daring,
    plunged for the highest cluster
        and anyone elsewhere was sanctioned to hoop

while the colander parties jammed and pruned,
    blocking the ring-road and corso.
        And into the shadows you went to gather

their younger voices, wiped from the tape
    when the hollows under the foam were rewired
        and their blouses at shoulder height blued.

The sun has burned all the dormouse day
    and you have only the swifts above,
        the metallic alarm of a mothering blackbird

in your ear. Of what do the decades consist?
    If no one asks me I know: a digger up to its oxters
        in roses, the woodpigeon's clap and glide,

the spill as of sand and the red berries passing
    the double-slit of your eyes, Mnemosyne:
        queen of the patterns on a darkening wall.

HORTUS CONCLUSUS

for Màiri

Her reflection inclosed, bathing molten and blue,
flowers without a shadow: now the weeping child
will sleep and the glinting heads of floorboard nails
climb through the timber sky.

IN THIS WAY

after Yves Bonnefoy

In this way our footprints follow
through the ruins of giant clouds –
a torn down blue that can be
only distant blue, the ground
vivid as sunlight
on the shoulder of a hill. Look
at the mud, you say,
as we tread its vast holdings, death's
lantern igniting our footprints from below.
In this way, alight, we follow.

*Foolish darkness, pressing its face
to the panes*

SETTLEMENT

We are neozoa, packed in lodgings
builder-owners quit with cart and hound
bequeathing as they scattered hence
the riddling gifts they held in song –
the *old man's face*, the *dyers' rock*,
a *well of sunken swords*, the place
where three streams meet. Their sounds
beguile us still, whispers from the cave
where kings and broken outlaws hid.

High water blackened the sand: it happened
on the day my face burned raw and box-
crabs in their thousands crossed the wall.
I remember how my blistered fingers paled
and each man clenched a wooden haft,
the keel's fleet shadow in the sunlit depths,
strangely flickering on and off the silt,
inscribed our own ungrounded tenure here,
and translucent fronds, fan-shaped and pink,
flaunted mockery's giant wingbeat
in the equivocal flux. I fled along the shore,
perplexed on hearing two from who
knows where were walking along the road
with sweet hands joined. Their secret
tongue had touched my ear, a wedding
havocked thought could not endure.

FIVE RAW

I SUITCASE

Out on the lawn in the pouring rain
the sky hangs leaden overhead,
to my right a mighty pine,
on my left the apple, fecund:
such rosy fruit I shared with mine.
I do not lie out here in bed.
The landing window through the blur
contains you walking down the stair,
& someone else comes down I fear
who is not there with you but here.
There is no other place to go.
Wherever that is hurts us so.
I'll be this suitcase: jocund.

II RHYMES WITH FLYING

The old gent sat in front of the telly,
his brain sagged like a worn-out welly.
No, no, it's because of the rain
he cannot help himself & leaks.
He cannot stride along the river
humming rhymes against the weather,
& when he asks for his favourite dish
they bring instead this putrid mush.
Between the mouthfuls he forgot
who we folk were, and so to his cot
we gave him up and left him lying.
His eyes fixed on the sky in his window:
how can I know if that is a crow
when nothing in it rhymes with flying?

III EARTHWORKS

Nothing keeps changing & neither
lets the other gain ground. Four plates
go down & everybody is wrong.
We wait for the knives to come out;
the board is hexed with dry blood,
entrails blistered by fire. Anger
hurries a-gallop into the debatable space.
Serrated & pitiless now it will try the final
marches – pike, trench and palisade,
your motte-and-bailey, my scythe,
the downfall of shadow on a child's cheek.
Later, your leg bridges my hip,
the din of battle wanes. Foolish
darkness, pressing its face to the panes.

IV THE SKIP OF STUFF

She'd been gazing into the yard of late
at a far-flung triangle in the darkness
three floors down. There
her geometric community mingled: the inmates'
windows, unceasingly lit or
obscure, riddling the flagged earth.
Her kitchen was once a tidy empire,
her domestic round – rapine has descended
since on all its shelves & machines,
their bare skin soiled. In the corner
someone has left a pile of linoleum tiles.
As we sweep the floor the sun sinks
over the fields, its sphere for a moment
emblazoned on a cupboard door.

v The Little Egret

Come along the river & we'll finish
the job. One shelf of thrillers
& a wooden cross: into the skip.
Lop the magnolia's branches off,
later sell the trunk. Doubtless
we shall dream of things that wear
this cruelly with our early years. You saw
the little egret settle in the stubble
by the lake? What shall we live for
now? The surface we barely inhabit,
watery, grey – sublimities here and there.
All of this can be scrubbed. The voices
in the furrow are no longer ours –
a slow wing beat as we go.

SKEW

The day was dark and slanting rain in ropes
hung from the sky – the gabled cloud as always sealed
the soft stone terre-à-terre.

I turned to the opening west and saw
those bands of shadow drawn across the grey beyond,
the water's mass evanishing in air.

As if against indifference their firmer hue
rose up against the river mouth – that fjord, channel,
sound, the straits of anywhere:

a little row of flats, the transverse
gradients of waves were cables taut between their posts,
and still the sky remained – a shield, the arch obscure.

STELLAR STATE

If the valley fills with water, if the valley
fills with light, if the stars can trip our gaze
so surely, surely they can stay till May.
Stellata if you leave my bedside
while I watch the water rise, if the air
grows damp, if we are sinking, if my sight
will see no person pass alone
but clouds and showers, window days,
a garden, tree, the petals burning
blind, then nothing here but white

HOMAGE TO DEMOCRITUS

And went down to the lowest step
to study what exists – the godless *hyle*,
her children's game of congruous bricks,
of hooking block to numberless block
to match the crumbling idols in the sky,
but saw my fingers in the grit and froth,

her hand palm-upward on the earth,
pale shoulder turning, mine consenting
like the dove with dove – this cheer of similars,
the very force that grew the material world
when out of uncuttable, spiralling showers
conjoining solids, aspirant, teemed forth.

Atoms and the empty space are all that is,
unceasingly inclined to a swing and chime –
thus the water in the river washes water,
pebbles of a like size roll together,
in the meadow crane stands next to crane.
The rest is just convention: sweet and bitter.

SIGNS, GAMES AND MESSAGES

for György Kurtág

Barbels hang like logs along the reeds –
their stillness is an ancient music heard
before the sound he wants to make begins.
The master walks beside the water
while his students rest (the cellist
under orders bows *a creaking door*).
When he reaches halfway round the lake
a stone flies through the air.
The water surface bends but does not tear.
Gathered on the other bank the children
clap and shout to Kurtág György,

who waves and listens to his prelude sing
as silent notes resound beneath the skin.

A MARINER OF MAN

So I have lacked a place to be nostalgic about,
but I've gone on hoping to find one.
                                                FRANK KERMODE

He was here on the Wednesday
waiting beneath my window
a pipe between his lips
not a minute after nine.

Someone had said a woman,
slim waist, over her shoulder
a quiver, would meet him on the shore.
Her forehead shone in the swell

flying fish skimmed
over the coral deep –
and still her ship held off.
We had taken a house by the sea

yet he spoke of a journey home.
The sky thickened with swifts.
He was laughing in the dark
but the waves did not reply.

He saw the house grow smaller –
his watered rum on the board –
the brimstones' dance on the ivy –
the gleaming clasp at her breast –

COLUMBA

for Quercus37

What will the morning bring?
A wood pigeon's call
in a late summer's garden
so long ago?

What quartering memory has found
is not the dove but the oak
at the edge of a lawn, the goalposts
long out of use.

                          Beyond

were rows that stretched
to stunted elms, the yew, a path
that led through a gap in the wall
to links and the open sea.

But soon the restless pigeon too
must have flown to a different land –
the view of it splintered, its voice
unbodied and sheer.

                         Something

is reaching down
through the skylight, leaving us
used for a moment longer
in this endlessly turning cell.

GRAVEYARD BY THE SEA

The doves float and red keels
mottle the ink-fretted waves,
over the roofs come straining sails
and pilgrims file through the gate.

Walking the wall you light
on the carcass of a dog, your eye
picks over its wasted hide
and slides into bone-thick sleep.

The minutes flood with years.
Emptied by their sojourns in the rain
the pages crackle in the breeze.

TRANSLATOR'S NOTE

But nothing's lost. Or else: all is translation
And every bit of us is lost in it
JAMES MERRILL

In the beginning
there was only the empty road
ahead, mist, the dead
of winter branching
into fields of snow
(say it another way:

close to the dying
branch in the road
waited the buried
trove, dung, the fount
under hoar-frosted elms):
on this fickle trail

our travellers gathered too
stamping their feet,
and the small hours –
copper between the branches –
flipped like pennies
to shadow the eyes.

The ice in the shallows
flounders and clicks.
O is the note
I've entered for the ghosts,
and now we may watch it
rolling along

this tow-path
like an empty ducat, misty-white.
It says: 'trust me, reader,

trust me not'.
Or consider this:
I saw a crow

with a small fish, a spot
of blood where the path
forked and the slopes
were forever verging
on white
across the outer edge.

(O is the fringe,
the margin, the snowy ridge).
Distance makes
the fish grow feet –
and like the hours the fish-folk
entered once upon the world,

and how hard that is
to grasp. We wait
at the crossroads: more coins
come flying, sledge rides
with children, the ever-
deepening snow. Muck-

rakers chide our beacons
of simile – their distant shore
is murk. We may have reached
the place, may not. On every
roof a sparrow hocks,
whistling as never before.

Iain Galbraith was born in Glasgow and grew up in the village of Arrochar / Argyll on the west coast of Scotland. After training in hotel management he studied languages and literature at the universities of Cambridge, Freiburg and Mainz. His poems have appeared in many journals and anthologies, including *Poetry Review, New Writing, The Times Literary Supplement, PN Review, Edinburgh Review* and *Irish Pages,* also in translation in German and Austrian journals, such as *Sinn und Form, Akzente or Manuskripte.* This is his first book of poems.

He is also an essayist and translator of poetry, fiction and drama, and has won several prestigious prizes for his work, including the Stephen Spender Prize, the Popescu European Poetry Translation Prize and the Schlegel-Tieck Prize.

He now lives in Wiesbaden, Germany.